Piggy Bank
Planning

Michelle Jovin, M.A.

Consultant

Chrissy Johnson, M.Ed.
Elementary School Teacher
Cedar Point Elementary

Publishing Credits

Rachelle Cracchiolo, M.S.Ed., *Publisher*
Aubrie Nielsen, M.S.Ed., *EVP of Content Development*
Emily R. Smith, M.A.Ed., *VP of Content Development*
Véronique Bos, *Creative Director*
Robin Erickson, *Art Director*
Michelle Jovin, M.A., *Associate Editor*
Lee Aucoin, *Senior Graphic Designer*

Image Credits: p.7 Library of Congress [LC-DIG-nclc-04991]; all other images from iStock and/or Shutterstock.

Library of Congress Cataloging-in-Publication Data
Names: Jovin, Michelle, author.
Title: Piggy bank planning / Michelle Jovin, M.A.
Description: Huntington Beach, CA : Teacher Created Materials, [2020] |
    Includes index. | Audience: Grades 2-3 | Summary: "Every day, we decide
    what to do with our money. How much should we save? How much should we
    spend? Learn more about how to make these tough decisions!"-- Provided
    by publisher.
Identifiers: LCCN 2020000693 (print) | LCCN 2020000694 (ebook) | ISBN
    9781087606385 (paperback) | ISBN 9781087618890 (ebook)
Subjects: LCSH: Money--Juvenile literature.
Classification: LCC HG221.5 J69 2020 (print) | LCC HG221.5 (ebook) | DDC
    332.024--dc23
LC record available at https://lccn.loc.gov/2020000693
LC ebook record available at https://lccn.loc.gov/2020000694

TCM | Teacher Created Materials

5482 Argosy Avenue
Huntington Beach, CA 92649
www.tcmpub.com
ISBN 978-1-0876-0638-5

Table of Contents

Choices

Every day, people make choices. They choose what to wear. They choose what to eat. And they choose what to do with their money.

Some people choose to save their money and not spend it. Other people spend money by buying things. People may not realize it at the time, but these choices **affect** their lives.

Helping Others

People spend money when they buy things. They spend money in other ways too. Many people give money to others who need help.

Earning Money

Before you can decide what to do with your money, you have to earn it! In the United States, states have **laws** that stop children from working. Instead, their job is to go to school.

Laws make it so children can focus on learning. These laws try to keep children from feeling **stress** about making money. Still, even without jobs, young people can earn money. They just have to get **creative**.

Children with Jobs

The U.S. government suggests that children should not work until they are at least 14 years old. Even then, there are laws to keep children safe. This has not always been true. Long ago, children often worked dangerous jobs.

Some young people earn allowances. That is money earned for doing **chores** or other tasks. Other young people might help their neighbors. They can rake leaves, shovel snow, or wash cars for extra cash.

The first step in making money is to ask adults for help. They can tell you what jobs you can and cannot do.

Other Types of Pay

Most children earn cash for chores. But that is not the only way they can be paid. They might earn other rewards. They might get to stay out late one night or have a sleepover. These things are not cash, but they still have **value**.

Saving Money

Once you have earned money, you can decide what to do with it. Your two main options are to save it or to spend it. To save money, you can store it in a bank. The bank will keep your money safe.

You can also save your money at home. You can store it in a safe place, like a jar or a piggy bank. Then, when you need to buy something, your money is close by.

How Much to Save

When you are young, you do not have a lot of things that you need to pay for. So, you can spend or give away more money than you save. As you get older, try to save more and spend less.

Savings Goals

Saving money is important. It will help you plan for your future. It will also help you buy things that are more expensive. Once you start saving money, you should set a goal for yourself. Think of something that you would like to buy or do. Learn how much it costs. That amount will be your goal. Having a goal in mind will help you decide how much to save and how much you can spend.

Save More, Spend Less

Imagine that you earn $20 each
month. You spend $5 and save
the other $15. After one year,
you will have saved $180!

Short-Term Goals

If what you want does not cost a lot of money, you will not have to save for long. Maybe you want to buy a toy. Or maybe you want to go to the movies. It will not take a long time to save up enough money for those things. These types of goals are called short-term goals. That is because it only takes a short amount of time before you reach your goal.

Different Goals

To go to the movies, you might need around $15. But a new video game can cost much more. So, the amount you save will change based on what you need or want.

Long-Term Goals

Short-term goals are great for things that do not cost a lot of money. But what if you want something that is expensive? Then, you will have to save for a lot longer. These goals are called long-term goals.

Long-term goals can be hard to achieve. You may not want to save for as long as you need to. But keep reminding yourself why you set the goal. That will help you stay interested in your plan.

Making a Plan

Planning for a long-term goal can be tricky. Decide how much it will cost and when you want to buy the item. Then, make a plan. Imagine you want to go to a concert. Your ticket will cost $30. So, you know to save $5 each month for the next six months.

Setting a Budget

Once you have set your goal, you should make a **budget**. A budget is a plan for how you will save and spend money. When you make your budget, think of money you earn. That gets added to your total. Money you plan to save and spend will be subtracted the amount of cash you have left. You can decide whether to save or spend the leftover cash.

If you stick to your budget, you will see your **progress** toward your goal. Each time you save money, you get closer to your goal. That makes it easier to stick to your plan.

SAVE

SPEND

BUDGET

earn	$20
lunch	-$5
save in jar	-$5
left to spend	$10

A Sample Budget

Imagine that you earn $20 each month for walking your neighbors' dogs. You know you will spend $5 on lunch. You put aside another $5 in your budget to save. That means you have $10 left to spend each month. Making a budget will help you not to overspend.

Spending Money

Once you have reached your goal, you may choose to keep saving. Or you may choose to spend what you have earned.

If you want to buy something, do **research** first. See where you can get the best deal. It may be at a local store, or it may be online. Study your options before you spend. That will help you make the most of your money.

Making Choices

When you have saved a lot of money, it may seem fun to spend it all. But if you do, you will have to start saving all over again. If you keep some money, it will be easier to meet your next goal.

Buying Goods

The things people buy fall into one of two categories—goods or services. Goods are things you can hold or touch. You can hold a bracelet and touch a house. Both of those things are goods people can buy. Video games, bikes, and clothes are all goods too.

Consumers and Producers

When you buy things, you are called a consumer. To *consume* something means to take or use it. People who make the things you buy are called producers. They *produce*, or make, things for others.

Paying for Services

You can also pay for services. Services are things that you pay other people to do for you. One example of a service is when an adult pays for day care. That is a service because the adult is paying someone to watch their children for them.

You can pay someone to cut your hair. You can pay a dentist to check your teeth. And you can pay a doctor to check your health. These are all services you can pay for.

Other Ways to Pay

Some people **trade** for services instead of paying. For example, you might have a friend who knows how to fix a flat tire on a bike. You could offer to draw them a picture if they help you. Your picture is how you will pay for their service.

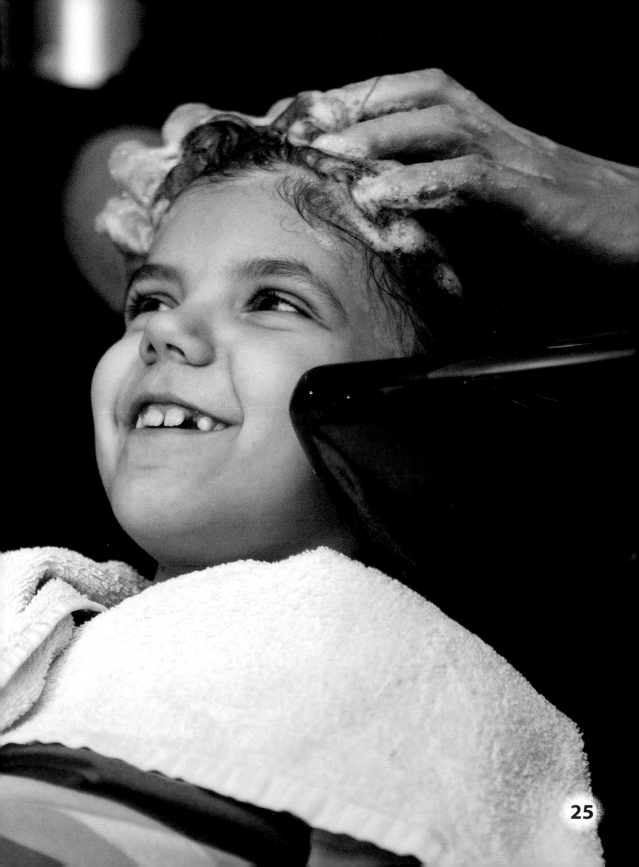

Making Decisions

It can be hard to decide what to do with your money. Most of the time, it is more fun to spend money than to save it. And saving up to buy an expensive item can take a long time. But you will feel proud when you reach your goals.

The next time you earn money, think about your choices. It can be hard to decide what to do. Having a plan in place will make those choices a lot easier.

Giving Things Up

When you choose what to do with your money, you give things up. By saving money, you give up buying something. By buying something, you give up the money you have saved. Know your options and choose the best path for you.

Remember It!

It can be hard to save money. You might see something you want to buy. You might even forget why you started saving in the first place!

Think of something you would like to pay for. Set a short-term goal or a long-term goal for saving money. Decide what you are willing to give up to save for it.

Come up with a way to remind yourself of your goal. You may want to write a song that you can sing to yourself. Or draw a picture of yourself meeting your goal. Then, put your creation in a place where you can see it often.

Your Goal!

$45

Glossary

affect—change or have an impact

budget—a plan for using money

chores—tasks done in or around the house

creative—showing or using imagination to come up with new and original things

laws—rules in communities

progress—movement and growth toward a goal

research—a careful study that is done to get more information

stress—worry

trade—give something to get something else

value—importance or worth

Index

Your Turn!

Banks are safe places to keep your money. Sometimes, though, it can be helpful to have money nearby that is not in the bank. Draw a design for a place to keep your money nearby, such as a piggy bank. You can draw it as a pig or choose any other shape you want. Then, build your own bank!